UnLonely

UNLONELY

An Hachette UK Company
www.hachette.co.uk

Summersdale Publishers Ltd
Part of Octopus Publishing Group Limited
Carmelite House
50 Victoria Embankment
LONDON
EC4Y 0DZ
UK

www.summersdale.com

Printed and bound in China

ISBN: 978-1-78783-544-3

Substantial discounts on bulk quantities of Summersdale books are available to corporations, professional associations and other organizations. For details contact general enquiries: telephone: +44 (0) 1243 771107 or email: enquiries@summersdale.com.

UnLonely

How to Feel
Less Isolated,
Make Connections
and Live a
Life You Love

Claire Chamberlain

INTRODUCTION

It's an unfortunate fact of life that everybody feels lonely sometimes. You may be able to take some comfort from knowing you're not the only one feeling this way. Loneliness can strike anybody and, contrary to popular belief, you may not even be alone when you experience these feelings of disconnection from others – sometimes, a crowded room can feel like the loneliest place in the world. Loneliness can be deeply uncomfortable and distressing, but, if you can put some self-care measures in place, shift your perspective from one of loneliness to solitude and take some simple steps to connect with those around you on a deeper, more meaningful level, you can begin to find solace in the fact it will not last forever.

If you've found your way to this book because you're going through a difficult period for whatever reason, I hope that it offers you reassurance, support and practical inspiration, so you start feeling more confident about connecting with others and able to build a close, supportive network around yourself.

What a lovely surprise to finally discover how unlonely being alone can be.

Ellen Burstyn

What is loneliness?

Loneliness is not a pleasant feeling, and yet it's something we have undoubtedly all experienced from time to time. You can feel lonely in a variety of different situations, from being physically alone, to being surrounded by others and yet feeling like you don't really fit in. Whatever your experience, you will likely identify with the fact that lacking close human interaction can leave you feeling disconnected somehow. And it's this disconnection that can make you feel isolated, unhappy and lonely.

7

LONELINESS IS
A PERCEPTION

Of course, not everyone who spends a lot of time alone is lonely. Loneliness is a perception, based on your own personal beliefs, desires and social needs. You might spend a large proportion of your day in solitude and yet feel perfectly secure, fulfilled and content. For some, the peace and quiet of being alone might be a joy, providing them with the silence needed to think and the space to throw themselves into creative projects. If this is the case, then loneliness will simply not be part of the equation. However, if your circumstances mean you spend large portions of your life alone and you actually crave human connection, then loneliness is likely to play an important part in your experience. The degree to which you experience loneliness is entirely personal and will be unique for everyone.

LONELINESS
AND EVOLUTION

Collectively as a species, we have evolved to seek out close human interaction. This makes sense when you think about it – in days gone by, we had to stick together in order to ensure our survival, living in tribes, working as a team by taking on specific roles within our societies, and sharing our stories and experiences with others. This need for connection is therefore hardwired into our DNA. We need to form close bonds with others in order to feel secure, for when we feel understood and as though we belong as part of a group, we feel safe. Conversely, feeling as if we are on the edge of society – that we don't belong – leaves us uneasy, unsettled and, primarily, unhappy. All of which can be explained from an evolutionary point of view, too – if we live on the periphery of society, our survival suddenly becomes uncertain, as we lack protection.

People are never too young or too old to look for human connection.

John Turturro

You're not the only one

As much as it can feel like you're entirely alone and that no one understands how you feel, every person on the planet has experienced loneliness at some point in their lives. No one feels like they fit in all the time and no matter how confident others may outwardly appear, everyone knows what it feels like to be "the outsider".

NOT ALONE,
BUT LONELY

Often when we picture loneliness, we imagine being physically all on our own. However, it's perfectly possible to be surrounded by other people and yet still feel lonely. For example, you could be at home by yourself, curled up on the sofa with a cup of hot tea and a good book, and feel perfectly happy and at ease. On the other hand, you might be at a party surrounded by a large group of acquaintances and yet feel utterly alone. Often, it comes down to how much we feel understood and accepted by those around us, and how connected we feel on a level that's deeper than "small talk". If we don't have a true connection with a person or group of people, or if our confidence is low at that moment, meaning we're not in the best place to form new relationships, it's perfectly possible to feel alone in a crowd. It's natural to be unsettled by this and allow the loneliness to feed feelings of low self-worth, but remember, this situation does not dictate who you are: it's just one moment.

Loneliness and physical health

While loneliness is not a medical condition in itself, it can pose a threat to your long-term physical health. In a 2015 study by Holt-Lunstad, social isolation was found to be as damaging to your health as smoking 15 cigarettes a day, with loneliness increasing the risk of everything from high blood pressure, coronary heart disease and stroke, to physical disability and mortality – a sobering fact and one that demonstrates the importance of human connection.

Loneliness and mental health

While the impact of loneliness on your physical health may come as a shock, it is probably no surprise that feeling lonely impacts your mental health. In fact, research suggests that loneliness and poor mental health are intrinsically linked. If you regularly experience feelings of loneliness, you might be more susceptible to certain mental health problems, including anxiety and depression. If you're feeling lonely, it might also be affecting your confidence and sense of self-worth.

LONELINESS EXPRESSES THE PAIN OF BEING ALONE AND SOLITUDE EXPRESSES THE GLORY OF BEING ALONE.

Paul Tillich

Modern-day loneliness

Researchers have long observed that chronic loneliness (feeling lonely for a prolonged period of time) is becoming something of a modern-day epidemic. In a world in which many of us live far from extended family, work remotely and spend more time "socializing" online than in the real world, it's no wonder that our sense of connection with others is diminishing. The good news is that, with a little effort and a few lifestyle changes, it's perfectly possible to rebuild a sense of community.

Technology and interaction

There's no doubt that advances in technology have revolutionized our lives – but not always for the better. We now spend far more of our time interacting via technology, whether that's working, shopping, messaging on social media or dating. While these online interactions are convenient and feel like they are keeping us in touch with the real world, the lack of face-to-face contact makes this type of communication far more superficial and ultimately less fulfilling, often leaving us feeling more isolated and alone.

As connected as we are with technology, it's also removed us from having to have human connection, made it more convenient to not be intimate.

Sandra Bullock

THE "SOCIAL"
MEDIA
CONUNDRUM

The introduction of social media into our lives has placed a huge question mark over what it means to be "social" in modern-day society. On the face of it, social sites such as Facebook, Twitter, Instagram and Pinterest have broadened our horizons when it comes to engaging with others, allowing us to stay connected and interact with people 24/7. But behind this interactive facade, researchers are discovering a very different story. In fact, many studies are finding that high social media use actually makes us feel lonelier, with one 2017 study, published in the American Journal of Preventative Medicine, suggesting that if you spend more than two hours a day engaging with social media, your chances of feeling isolated in real life are twice as high as average. Perhaps people who are lonely are more likely to spend more time on social media in the first place, but other theories as to why this is the case point to higher levels of FOMO (fear of missing out) and the very real fact that online encounters are simply not a substitute for the closeness of real-life, meaningful connection.

WHAT IS FOMO?

If you find yourself constantly checking your phone to scan other people's photos and updates, saying yes to every single invite or request and always feeling anxious that other people are having more exciting and fulfilling experiences than you are, you may well be suffering from FOMO. A very real phenomenon, FOMO is described as apprehension felt by thinking other people might be engaged in rewarding activities and experiences, while you are not. This perception of being "left out" can be incredibly emotionally painful and consequently make you feel desperate to stay constantly connected to what others are doing, often via social media. While worrying that you're being left out is certainly nothing new, in recent decades it has become amplified by social media, and our "always-on" society can make you feel like everyone else is always out having a good time, when the reality is that is simply not the case. If you recognize the characteristic traits of FOMO in yourself, it might be a good idea to remind yourself that social media is not real life – it's merely the best bits of other people's days that they are happy and willing to share.

Suddenly lonely

Feelings of loneliness creep in for everyone at certain times of life. It might be short-term – for example, when you suddenly find yourself alone on Sunday evening after a busy weekend with friends. Or it might be because of a more specific life change, such as breaking up with a partner. Whatever the reason, loneliness can take you by surprise and thrust you into a sea of difficult emotions. But take a deep breath: these feelings won't be this all-encompassing forever. The following pages detail just some of the scenarios that can result in you feeling all alone...

Moving home

Whether you're moving to the next town or a completely different country, moving home can be a stressful experience. And if you're moving away from friends, family and a community that you have been a part of for a long time, it can quickly result in feelings of isolation and loneliness. Keeping in contact with old friends with regular phone calls and visits (if possible) can help. It's also a good idea to begin integrating into your new community as soon as possible, too – after all, it's now your home! Introducing yourself to neighbours is a great way to start.

GOING TO
UNIVERSITY

Heading away from home for the first time to attend college or university can be daunting. On the one hand, you're entering a new period of your life, filled with the opportunity to meet lots of new people, yet on the other, you are leaving behind all that is familiar. The pressure to make new friends and have fun can bring with it anxiety, and worries about not "fitting in" can increase feelings of insecurity. The fact is that, while this time of your life is billed as being an exciting chance to gain independence, it's perfectly normal to experience feelings of uncertainty and loneliness. If you're struggling to adapt, know that you are not the only one and there are people around who can help. Joining clubs can be a good way to meet like-minded people, or why not look into volunteering options on campus or in the local area? Check out your Students' Union for advice. Making a concerted effort to chat with others in common rooms or kitchens can help to boost your confidence, and there will be counselling services you can utilize, too, for professional support.

WORKING ALONE

The opportunity to work remotely (or for yourself) offers some fantastic benefits, including being able to work at home in your pyjamas. But there can be drawbacks, not least the increased likelihood of experiencing loneliness, since you don't have instant daily interaction with others, and having to make a conscious effort to connect with other people regularly. If this sounds familiar, there are things you can do.

Is it possible to hold Skype meetings or FaceTime catch-ups with colleagues? It's not quite the same as meeting in person, but it can be the next best thing. Ensure you get outside daily and chat to at least one other person – a neighbour or shop assistant, for example. Connection with others doesn't always have to be deep – even a short interaction can go a long way to alleviate feelings of isolation. Take advantage of flexible hours to attend daytime events or clubs to encourage you to leave the house more often. And, if you find the quietness of having no colleagues around oppressive, try putting the radio on – a simple tip but one that can make you feel less alone.

BREAKING UP
WITH A PARTNER

There's no way around the fact that break-ups can be hard, especially if you had been with your partner for a long period of time. Even if you know a split is for the best, the sudden isolation that comes from not having another person around, particularly in the evenings, can be painful. When someone else has made up a large portion of your life, you can be left feeling vulnerable and disconnected when they are gone. This can lead you to try to numb the pain, for example with alcohol, or make you feel that you immediately need to get back "out there". But try to use this time to reflect upon what will really be good for you in this moment. If you're lonely, it can be tempting to start dating again straight away (and if this feels right, then by all means do!). However, you might find that, after a lengthy relationship with someone, now is a good time for some reflection and self-care: go for an invigorating walk, take a bath, watch whatever you want on TV, spend time with good friends and don't rush any potential next steps.

Redundancy or retirement

Being out of work – whether it's expected or unexpected – is a big change and one that can leave you feeling unfulfilled and isolated. If you've spent much of your adult life performing a role within society, suddenly being unable to do that can create a sense of loss and detachment, even if it is something you have had time to prepare for. If you find yourself experiencing loneliness due to a break from work, seeking out voluntary or charitable opportunities can help to give you a sense of purpose and fulfilling connections with others.

Everyone on this planet has felt like this at some point

BECOMING
A PARENT

While having a baby brings with it much-anticipated joy and excitement, it can also be a difficult time for some, which is perfectly normal. If you have taken maternity or paternity leave from a job where you have daily adult interaction, suddenly being at home with a newborn can leave you feeling isolated, alone and overwhelmed. These feelings can often be exacerbated for the individual who is grappling with the demands of parenthood alone, either as a single parent or while their partner has to return to work (and "normality"). If you are feeling like this, it is time to seek help and support. Look for parent and baby groups, sign up to a class (you will often find free activities on offer at local libraries and church halls) or invite another new parent over for a coffee. Once you start chatting to others in the same situation, you will likely come across a few kindred spirits. If you find the idea of meeting others too overwhelming, feel yourself withdrawing from those around you, regularly become overwhelmed with anxious thoughts or are experiencing feelings of emptiness, speak with your health visitor or doctor.

Experiencing bereavement

The loss of a loved one is painful. While everybody handles grief in their own way, a common theme is a sense of loneliness, which slips into the empty space your loved one has left behind. Be gentle with yourself. There's no right or wrong way to feel or act, although bottling up your grief is likely to make things harder. Try opening up to a friend – sharing memories can be cathartic. You could also do something proactive in your loved one's memory, such as taking part in a fundraising event – this will give you something positive to focus on, and get you out and about.

Embracing alone time

When feelings of loneliness arise, your first thought might be to seek out others, to help fill the void. But sometimes, by turning your attention inward – to your own needs and passions – you can learn to form a deeper and more meaningful connection with yourself, helping to transform your loneliness into a productive and far less frightening state: solitude. By using your time alone to pursue creative, fulfilling, enjoyable and fruitful activities, you may find that the deeper connection you were seeking was within you all along. The following pages offer up tips and ideas on how to embrace your time alone more fully...

Prioritize your well-being

When you're feeling lonely, it's easy to let the little things go and stop taking good care of yourself, both mentally and physically. But in order to remain (or return to feeling) positive, looking after yourself is important. Simple things like taking a hot shower each morning and using your favourite shower gel, picking an outfit that makes you feel good, enjoying a hot cup of tea, doing a spot of mindful colouring, getting out for some exercise and cooking yourself a tasty dinner each evening can go a long way to boosting your mood and your self-esteem.

I will show
myself love,
kindness and
acceptance

EXPRESS
GRATITUDE

Taking time each day to think about all that you have to be grateful for in your life has been proven to have a positive impact on almost all areas of life, including enhancing self-esteem, increasing optimism, boosting energy, deepening relaxation, promoting feelings of kindness, improving sleep quality and – crucially – strengthening social bonds. In short, expressing gratitude can alter your whole mindset, making you feel happier and more open to forming and developing relationships with those around you. In fact, a 2015 study published in Europe's Journal of Psychology found that loneliness and gratitude are negatively correlated, meaning that when feelings of gratitude are high, feelings of loneliness become low. A good way to start is to keep a daily gratitude journal. At the end of each day, list three (or more if you want!) things that you are most grateful for. After a month, take a moment to notice if this daily practice has changed your outlook at all.

Swap FOMO for JOMO

Feeling anxious and tired because of your FOMO? Then it's time to start embracing the joy of missing out (JOMO), instead! JOMO celebrates life at a slower, more deliberate pace. It's about accepting that you can't be part of everything all the time, turning your attention away from outside distractions (such as social media, which can leave you feeling anxious and overwhelmed) and instead living a more intentional, mindful life: one in which you truly relish the joy of settling on the sofa under a duvet in the evening, with a mug of hot chocolate and your favourite film on TV.

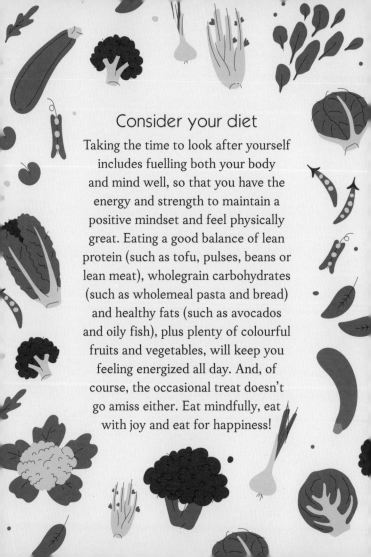

Consider your diet

Taking the time to look after yourself includes fuelling both your body and mind well, so that you have the energy and strength to maintain a positive mindset and feel physically great. Eating a good balance of lean protein (such as tofu, pulses, beans or lean meat), wholegrain carbohydrates (such as wholemeal pasta and bread) and healthy fats (such as avocados and oily fish), plus plenty of colourful fruits and vegetables, will keep you feeling energized all day. And, of course, the occasional treat doesn't go amiss either. Eat mindfully, eat with joy and eat for happiness!

Be more mindful

Mindfulness is the act of becoming consciously aware of the present moment exactly as it is, without judgement. Spending time focusing on your surroundings can help to ground you in the here and now, taking you firmly into the physical world and away from thoughts, worries and anxieties. Reconnecting in this way can help you feel more at one with the world. To get started, begin to notice your surroundings or your bodily sensations. If a thought arises that takes your mind away from "now", acknowledge it without judgement, then draw your attention back to the present moment.

There is peace within my mind, body and soul

TRY MEDITATION

Meditation is a wonderful way to combat feelings of loneliness and separation. It is the practice of training your attention and awareness by focusing on a particular object, thought or feeling, to help achieve inner peace and stillness. However, more than that, meditation is a means of looking within yourself and cultivating a sense of connection with an inner presence or source – a source that binds you to everything and everyone, all at once. In this way, many people find that when meditating, it is impossible to feel lonely – that the sense of "oneness" with everything around you removes feelings of isolation. Scientists have even proven this to be true: analysis of brain scans of meditating Tibetan monks showed the areas of the brain associated with feelings of social isolation cooled immensely. To begin a simple meditation practice, sit quietly with your eyes closed and focus on your breathing. There are many guided meditations available online to help with this. Even ten minutes of meditation a day can make a big difference to your well-being.

GET SOME
FRESH AIR
(EVERY DAY)

There are so many reasons why
stepping outside into the fresh air
each day is good for your mind,
body and soul. Research has
shown that regular walking can
boost both your mood and self-
esteem, while also easing feelings
of anxiety and depression, and
reducing stress levels. On top of
that, natural sunlight is a fabulous
mood booster – and it's a key
component for good health, too.

Vitamin D (produced by your body when your skin is exposed to the sun) helps to maintain healthy bones, teeth and muscles, and research has shown there's also a link between vitamin D and mental health, with decreased levels of the vitamin associated with low mood. And of course, getting out and about is also a great way to combat feelings of isolation and loneliness, giving you the opportunity to interact and connect with passers-by if you wish – even if it's just a friendly smile or nod hello.

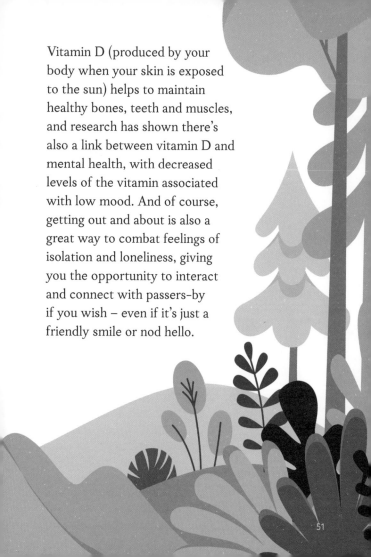

If you want to be happy, learn to be alone without being lonely. Learn that being alone does not mean being unhappy.

Michael Josephson

Lose yourself in a good book

There's nothing quite like diving into
the pages of a great book to help you
unwind and de-stress. Reading can help
you forget any worries or loneliness you
may be feeling, allowing you to enter
and inhabit a completely different world.
What's more, reading does not have to
be reserved for your home: carry a book
with you, so you can dip into it at any
convenient time when you might otherwise
feel lonely – while sitting in a coffee
shop or waiting for a train, perhaps. It's
far more enriching and rewarding than
scrolling through your smartphone!

Cook from scratch

If you live alone, it can be all too easy to fall into
the habit of eating ready meals or super-simple
suppers of an evening. But there is so much joy to
be had in flicking through recipe books, discovering
mouth-watering dishes, buying fresh ingredients
and taking your time preparing a delicious meal.
Making the effort to cook properly at least a
few times a week can feel so rewarding, and it
is a fabulous way to show yourself a little love.
Plus, you can freeze any leftovers and enjoy the
fruits of your labour again later in the week.

I APPRECIATE
EACH SMALL
MOMENT OF JOY
I EXPERIENCE

In order to be open to creativity, one must have the capacity for constructive use of solitude. One must overcome the fear of being alone.

Rollo May

Take up a hobby

Learning a new skill can give you a great sense of purpose and help you to feel more positive, as well as giving you the chance to connect with like-minded people. What would you really love to do that would spark joy and excitement? Think about your passions and interests: if you'd like to do something creative, there are so many possibilities out there, from watercolour painting and poetry writing, to pottery and piano lessons. Look for taster sessions or a beginner's course in your chosen activity and sign up!

Take a warm bath

Filling your hours alone with joyful self-care practices is a wonderful way to transform feelings of loneliness into an appreciation of solitude. Slipping into a warm bath is a great way to do this in the evening: dim the lights (or bathe by candlelight), add your favourite aromatherapy oil or bubble bath to the water and indulge in a well-deserved, relaxing soak.

Never be afraid to sit awhile and think.

Lorraine Hansberry

SPEND TIME
WITH ANIMALS

Many studies have demonstrated that the company of a pet can help to ease loneliness and can even lessen feelings of depression and low self-worth. The physical presence of a living creature undoubtedly provides comfort and, if you have the responsibility of caring for an animal – feeding, grooming and walking it – this interaction will likely improve your sense of self-worth and add a level of meaning to your life. While you can't have a two-way conversation with an animal, many people report feeling a deep sense of connection with their pets. And although you still undoubtedly need the presence of meaningful human interaction in your life to help alleviate social isolation, an animal can provide comfort and companionship. Pet ownership should never be entered into lightly, so if you are not in the position to care for an animal, find ways to interact with them outside of the home: feed the birds in your garden or the park; make time to stop and stroke the neighbour's cat; offer to walk a friend's dog one day a week; or enquire about volunteering at a local animal rescue centre.

Plant seeds

Growing a plant from seed can be hugely heart-warming and fulfilling, and you really don't need lots of space to do so. Even if you don't have a garden, plants can be grown on balconies and windowsills (in fact, if you have them inside your home, they will brighten up your living space and have even been shown to improve indoor air quality). All you need is a plant pot, some compost, seeds of your choice (which you can pick up from garden centres or supermarkets, or order online) and a little patience. Edible options are rewarding: try herbs and tomatoes.

I AM **CONNECTED**
TO **EVERYONE**
AND **EVERYTHING**
IN THE
NATURAL WORLD

Indulge in a duvet day

If you're sitting at home feeling lonely, try turning your mood around by intentionally creating a nurturing self-care duvet day. Put your phone to one side (or better still, switch it off), so you won't lose hours mindlessly scrolling, then set out your plans for an indulgent, guilt-free lazy day. Have a relaxing shower, pop on some clean comfortable pyjamas, do a jigsaw or get out your paints, pick out some feel-good movies, treat yourself to some popcorn and revel in the fact you have nowhere else you need to be right now.

You're always with
yourself, so you might as
well enjoy the company.

Diane von Furstenberg

TAKE UP EXERCISE

Make time for regular exercise in your life, and prove to yourself that your mental and physical health are a priority. The amazing benefits of boosting your fitness go far beyond improved physical strength and toning: countless studies have shown that physical exercise that raises your heart rate is proven to reduce stress, alleviate anxiety, ease mild to moderate depression and boost feelings of happiness, serenity and self-worth. It's all to do with the release of endorphins (feel-good hormones) into your bloodstream during and after exercise – and it's very hard to stay stuck in negative thoughts about loneliness and isolation when you're on a joyful exercise high. Choose a fitness pursuit that appeals to you (if it's something you find exciting, then you will be more likely to stick with it) and then plan your fitness sessions into your diary. Running, brisk walking, swimming and yoga are all accessible options, as you don't need much specialist kit to get started – just a little strength of mind and perseverance – but if you're drawn to them, why not look for a class in circus skills, rock climbing, water sports or dance classes?

Get an early night

It's easy to get into the habit of staying up late scrolling through other people's social media status updates or mindlessly watching TV into the early hours – neither of which are good for your self-esteem or general mental health. Setting an intention to step away from electronic devices and instead take care of yourself by getting to bed at a reasonable time will provide so many benefits, including helping your body to heal, recharge and reset, ready for the following day. Struggle to sleep? Try an online guided sleep meditation before you climb into bed, and avoid caffeine from mid-afternoon onward.

I inhale
slowly and
exhale
deeply, finding
peace in
each breath

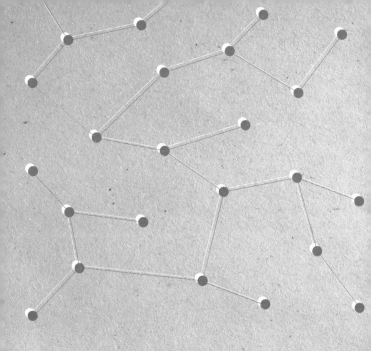

BOOST YOUR HUMAN
CONNECTIONS

While upping your self-care routine and taking steps to do things that fill you with joy will give your mental health a big boost and hopefully help to transform moments of unhappy loneliness into ones of reflective or creative solitude, the most proactive thing you can do to tackle feelings of isolation and loneliness is to increase your human interaction. Forming genuine, deep and meaningful connections with others is a sure-fire way to see your feelings of loneliness diminish – but it will take time and courage. Seeking social connection can be nerve-wracking at first, but the benefits will far outweigh any anxieties you may be experiencing. Remember, loneliness isn't a medical condition in itself. It is a symptom – a pain that helps you notice that something in your life isn't quite as you would like it to be. The following pages are packed with tips and advice on how to start forming bonds – both small and strong – with others.

I WILL LET MY STRENGTH AND POSITIVITY SHINE THROUGH TODAY

Start slowly

If you're feeling lonely and low in confidence, putting yourself in a situation that's ultimately going to make you feel nervous and uncomfortable probably isn't the best way to start forming connections with others. By all means, if you're confident about rocking up at a crowded bar all alone or heading to a friend of a friend's party by yourself, dive in and enjoy! But you really don't need to go in big right away. So, take a deep breath – there are lots of small ways you can connect with new people.

Smile at strangers

Make a point of smiling genuinely at people while you're out and about. Research has shown that smiling is actually contagious: people unconsciously mimic the facial expressions they see. What's more, smiling activates neural pathways in your brain, helping to boost feelings of happiness (this happens even if you're only smiling on the outside!). So smiling at someone – and being on the receiving end of their smile in return – will create a momentary connection with another person that will have positive benefits for you both. Good, eh?

This is the
perfect day
to smile at
everyone
I meet

We live in a world where
many of us have lots of friends
on Facebook but yet we have
lost human connection.

Robin Sharma

Sign up to an evening course

Look for a course to sign up to in your spare time. Choose something that fills you with excitement – this way, you'll be more likely to meet like-minded people. There are so many options, from book clubs and language courses, to art workshops and woodwork or DIY. Meeting people in this way can feel safe, because you're there to learn a specific skill, meaning that socially, the pressure is off. You can chat to others if you're feeling confident enough, or simply throw yourself into your newfound activity if you're not.

These days, technology has made it possible for us to go about our lives without ever interacting with another human being. Thanks to the prevalence of online shopping and self-checkouts in shops, there are far fewer opportunities for spontaneous chats and small talk. But this is such a shame: small talk, though small by name, has actually been proven to have big benefits, including boosting mental health (after all, just think how nice it is when someone says something kind to you) and being a precursor to potentially deeper connections. So when you're shopping, bypass automated transactions and make the effort to chat with staff at the checkout – they might brighten your day and you might brighten theirs.

Head to a coffee shop

If you find you're spending a lot of your time alone at home, or you work from home, heading out to a coffee shop for an hour can brighten your day and give you the chance to smile and interact with others. Even being close to others without interacting much can help you feel more connected to the outside world. So grab your journal or your sketchbook and treat yourself to a delicious hot drink while you watch the world go by.

We need to remind ourselves
of the beauty of human
connection and of nature and
pull ourselves out of devices for
a moment and appreciate what
it is just to be human beings.

Olivia Wilde

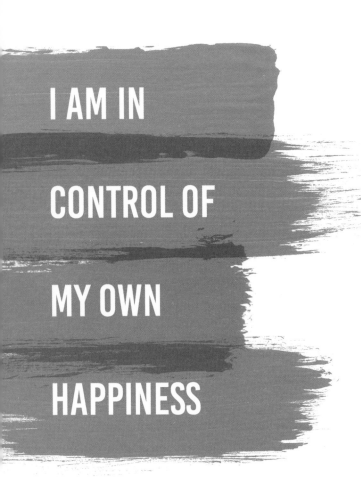

I AM IN

CONTROL OF

MY OWN

HAPPINESS

Enrol in a fitness class

As we've already mentioned, exercise is a great form of self-care, to help boost your well-being. And if you're looking to increase your social interaction, group exercise could be a great way to go. While you may not get to chat much during the class, there might be the chance for a quick exchange before or afterward (bonding over how much you ache is always a good start!). There are so many fun and challenging options to try... How about boxercise, spinning or Pilates?

TABLE
FOR ONE

Dining out alone can be extremely liberating, but even the most confident among us can feel daunted at the prospect of asking for a table for one. However, just because you don't have a dinner date doesn't mean you should miss out on delicious meals at nice restaurants – and it could be an exciting change from eating at home alone if that's what you're used to. Top tip: bring a good book with you. That way you can flit between people watching and getting lost in the pages if you start feeling anxious. It can also help make it less intimidating to book a table for one in advance, so you know you're guaranteed a spot. And scout out restaurants near you that have bar seating or small, cosy tables where you won't feel singled out for being on your own.

I AM
COMFORTABLE
IN MY OWN
COMPANY

Social media has given us this idea that we should all have a posse of friends when in reality, if we have one or two really good friends, we are lucky.

Brené Brown

GIVE YOUR FULL
ATTENTION

As you start forging more offline connections with others, it could be a good idea to start simultaneously limiting your online time, to give new friendships space to grow – especially when you're in company. If you were having a conversation with someone, you'd probably find it highly distracting and impolite if they kept checking their phone in front of you every few minutes while you were talking. Extend those you are with the same courtesy by keeping your phone out of sight. By giving someone your full attention, even if it's just for a short chat, you will enhance your chances of truly connecting with them and leaving a positive impression. The more you practise keeping your phone out of sight, the easier it will become to focus your attention on what's happening right in front of you.

Reconsider your online friends

If social media is making you unhappy, consider why this might be. It's important to feel like people are on your side, wanting you to do well. If you find that sometimes this isn't the case in your online world, perhaps it's time to reconsider your online connections. There's really no point in having hundreds of "friends" if their posts or comments make you feel bad about yourself. Unfollowing those who don't have your back can be a powerful and liberating move.

A fixation with connection with "friends" online comes with the risk of disconnection with friends waiting for you to be present in the offline world.

Craig Hodges

TODAY I WILL HEAD OFFLINE AND STEP OUTSIDE

Volunteer your time

Giving up your time to help others is a great way to get involved in community or charitable projects, and it will offer up a whole new social world. Whatever your interests, there's bound to be something you can get involved with. See if local animal charities need help; volunteer at a care home or dementia café; or perhaps your local community holds gardening sessions for communal areas, such as recreation grounds and parks. Whatever you choose, getting out of the house, interacting with others and making a positive difference is a surefire way to feel empowered, useful and connected.

Become passionate about a cause

Find a cause you can really get behind and not only will you be helping to call for positive action and change, you will also have the chance to meet local people who share your passion and beliefs. From environmental causes, to animal rights, to refugee support, to any number of charitable or political ventures, coming together with others to campaign peacefully will give you a strong sense of purpose and belonging, and you might even make some new friends along the way.

I'M READY TO FIND MY OWN UNIQUE TRIBE

Friendship is born at that moment when one person says to another, "What? You too! I thought I was the only one."

C. S. Lewis

Pay a compliment

An unexpected spontaneous kind word is one
of the simplest ways of starting a conversation
with someone new. By reaching out in this
way you demonstrate generosity and kindness,
and it could go on to spark a lengthier
conversation. At the very least, you will have
put a smile on someone's face and brightened
their day, so it's worth giving it a try.

BEFRIEND OTHERS

Spending time focusing on your own loneliness has the potential to set off a cycle of anxiety, depression and feelings of low self-worth... and the worse you feel about yourself, the less likely you are going to be to start taking proactive measures to combat your sense of social isolation. One way around this is to stop focusing on your own loneliness and start thinking of ways you can help others to feel less lonely. Statistics show that social isolation increases with age, and, for instance, in the UK alone, some 2 million people over the age of 75 live alone. Perhaps you could spend an hour or two a week volunteering in a residential care home, chatting to residents over a cup of tea, or lending a hand at a coffee morning for elderly people (find out if your local church or community centre hosts these). Perhaps a local soup kitchen needs a helping hand where you could offer your services? Spending time with others who could benefit from a friendly face and kind word could make the world of difference – to both them and you.

Nurture existing relationships

One of the easiest ways to reduce feelings
of loneliness, improve your connections and
in turn boost your happiness is to pay more
attention to the relationships in your life that
you have already formed. If you cherish and
nurture these connections, they will begin to
grow and flourish, deepening and strengthening
your social bonds. The following pages offer
ideas and ways that you could approach this...

Don't feel alone, because there is always someone out there who loves you more than you can imagine.

Anurag Prakash Ray

PRIORITIZE
COMMUNICATION

It sounds obvious, but being able to communicate well with others is so important when it comes to forging fulfilling relationships. Thankfully, if you're an introvert, this doesn't mean you have to be the life and soul of the party, or talk to anyone and everyone at a gathering. It includes making eye contact with others, or smiling at them; it means listening effectively and giving someone your full attention when they're talking to you; it involves asking questions. Next time you're with someone you're comfortable with, such as a friend or family member, don't be afraid to ask them how they are and truly engage with their answer. You might be surprised how much they open up if you start prioritizing meaningful communication, without the distractions of smartphones or other people.

Reconnect with old friends

Is there a person in your life who you wish you hadn't lost contact with? Someone who you had a genuine bond with and who made you feel brighter, happier and more understood? If you lost contact with that person purely due to circumstance, such as moving away or the busyness of everyday life, why not send them a message and invite them out for coffee and a catch-up? When you have a true connection with a friend, you will probably find that when you start communicating again, it will feel like they never went away.

I will break
down the barriers
I have built
around myself

Find your tribe

Being able to connect truly and
meaningfully with others on a deeper
level is the perfect antidote to loneliness.
You don't need this level of connection
with lots of people – often just one
or two will do. Find someone who
understands you, and you've found
a member of your unique tribe.

A friend is someone
who knows all about
you and still loves you.

Elbert Hubbard

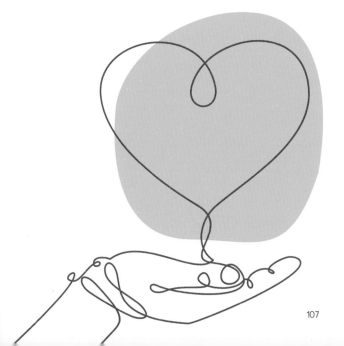

Make a phone call

In the age of Messenger, WhatsApp and Snapchat, it's easy to feel like you're connected with friends and family, without ever actually hearing their voices. Perhaps it's time to turn off the apps and pick up the phone (or FaceTime them), instead. It's not quite the same as chatting in person, but having a laugh together over the phone will help you feel more connected than typing endless messages.

Be curious

When you're talking with someone, pay attention
to what they're saying and show an interest in
them. By asking genuinely curious questions
and giving them the chance to open up and
show their true self, rather than trying to step
in and fill gaps in conversation with your own
stories, you will make them feel special and good
about themselves. Deep conversations can often
blossom into more meaningful connections.

I ACCEPT

this moment

EXACTLY

AS IT IS

Listen with intent

When we're having a conversation with someone, nerves and insecurities can often cause us to race ahead with ourselves. We're so keen to have something interesting or relevant to say that we're thinking of what our next sentence will be even as the other person is still talking. Because of this, we often don't truly hear what they are saying. The next time you're chatting with someone, give them space and truly listen to their words: it will make all the difference.

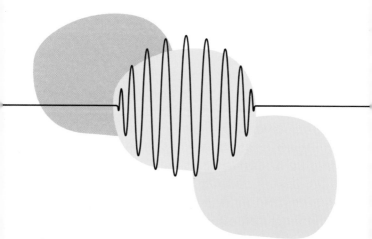

MAKE PLANS

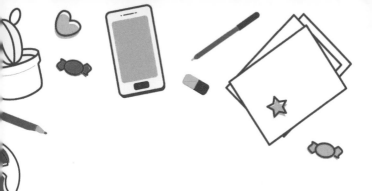

Don't be afraid to be the person who makes plans to meet up if other friends don't seem to get around to it. If you haven't heard from someone in a while, it can be easy to jump to the wrong conclusions about why, especially if you're feeling anxious or have been suffering with low self-esteem. Chances are, they have simply been busy with work, family or general life admin, and they would love to hear from you and catch up. So be brave and take that first step: send them a message asking how they are; ask if they'd like to meet for dinner one evening; offer to start looking into that weekend away you've always talked about but have never got around to arranging. Being proactive is a great way to get more meet-ups in your diary.

BE AUTHENTICALLY YOU

In an effort to "fit in" with those around you, it's common (and natural) to mimic other people's behaviour or pretend to be interested in the same things they are. But by hiding your true interests, likes and passions, all of a sudden you could find yourself hanging around with people who, while perfectly nice, don't share the same values as you, making true connection trickier. Never be afraid to be your own authentic self around others, even if letting your guard down is scary at first. True friends are the ones who share and appreciate your quirks and stick around – and you really only need one or two people who do that to feel understood and loved.

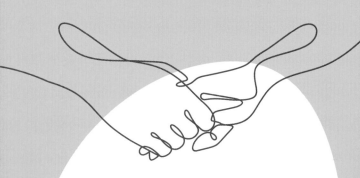

Practise compassion

Make sure you show yourself understanding,
especially when situations in life don't go
to plan. When you find yourself feeling
lonely or anxious, accept that this is not
your fault – that everyone feels this way
sometimes – and put in place some of
the self-care tips we covered earlier in
the book. Extend this compassion to
others, too: kindness, understanding
and forgiveness are the cornerstones of
any true friendship or connection.

You cannot be lonely
if you like the person
you're alone with.

Wayne Dyer

It can be scary telling someone else how you have been feeling, especially if the thoughts and emotions you've been experiencing have been ones of loneliness, anxiety, low mood, depression or low self-worth. But telling someone how you feel is often the most important step toward positive change. It's easy to assume that others will be able to tell how you are feeling, and in turn this can lead to resentment and further withdrawal: "How can they not see I'm feeling so alone and low? They must not care about me." On the contrary, generally people are so caught up in their own experiences and the busyness of everyday life that they simply haven't had time to stop and see that you're struggling. If your loneliness is becoming frequent, tell someone who cares about you: a close family member or friend, for example. It doesn't have to be a grand revelation: simply messaging them to let them know you could do with a chat, and asking them to call when they're free, is a light-hearted way to open up. Or arrange to meet for a coffee or a walk – somewhere you feel comfortable and won't be rushed.

Be genuinely
interested in everyone
you meet and everyone
you meet will be genuinely
interested in you.

Rasheed Ogunlaru

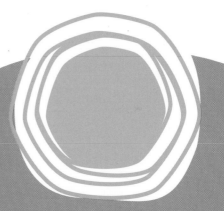

Tell people you appreciate them

Receiving a genuine compliment is heart-warming, so make sure you extend these compliments to others every now and again. Letting friends and family know how much you appreciate them and how glad you are that they are in your life is a wonderful way to honour the connection you share – and it will make you feel good, too. Shy about saying it to their face? Why not write down your appreciation in a card or email?

Taking responsibility for the relationships in your life is a hugely important step. In any relationship – whether it's personal or professional – you are jointly accountable for its health and strength. Every now and again, make an honest appraisal of your behaviour within your relationships. This can be uncomfortable, but it's important as it can reveal unconscious behaviours that may be preventing you from getting close to others. If you've been hurt before, have you been keeping other people at arm's length and not letting them in, to try to prevent it happening again? If you're shy, do you avoid eye contact or small talk with others, thereby not giving them the chance to connect or get to know you? How could you change this? Of course, this process works both ways: are there any relationships in your life that feel unhealthy? Do any of your friends make you feel used or unhappy? This is not OK. What steps could you take to address this? Sometimes, the answer might be to walk away. While painful, you will likely know in your gut whether it's the right choice or not.

Understanding your feelings

Loneliness can bring with it a host of painful emotions that you might be unwilling or unable to address. You might have started to believe that loneliness is just a part of who you are. But sustained periods of anxiety or low mood are not usual, and you deserve to feel happy. The following pages explore ways to better understand your emotions and feelings in relation to the loneliness you have been experiencing, as well as offering tips on how to cope and where you can find support and help...

I am
worthy
of love,
support
and
connection

Loneliness and emotions

It's important to acknowledge that
loneliness is often intrinsically linked with
feelings of anxiety, stress, low mood,
depression and low self-esteem. However,
sometimes it is hard to distinguish which
is the cause and which is the effect. If
you struggle with mental health issues,
loneliness can be a painful side effect of
this, but equally, feelings of loneliness are
likely to make you unhappy, anxious and
down. Taking time to understand your
feelings in relation to your loneliness can
help you find ways of managing your
sense of social isolation more effectively.

What is social anxiety?

Social anxiety disorder causes a person to feel intense fear, worry or stress when they are in certain (or all) social situations. It's not simply extreme shyness: it's a mental health problem that can have a big impact on your life, often leading to increased periods of isolation if help is not sought. Symptoms can include a dread of everyday activities such as speaking on the phone or shopping, low self-esteem, fear of criticism, and physical symptoms such as feeling sick or panic attacks. Social anxiety disorder can feel scary, but it's actually quite common and help is available – take the first step and visit your GP for a chat.

HOW DO
YOU LIKE TO
SOCIALIZE?

It's all very well deciding to tackle your loneliness by going to more social events, but if that's really not your thing, you probably aren't going to have the best time, and you will likely be left feeling vulnerable. Gaining a good understanding of your personality type can give you a better idea of your preferences when it comes to interacting with others. Think about the times you've felt happiest around others, and the times you've felt stressed, then note down a few details about the scenarios you were in. You might notice a theme: perhaps you feel comfortable with a certain person or group of friends but not others? Perhaps you prefer one-to-one meet-ups over large crowds, or vice versa? Or maybe having an activity to do, where the pressure to talk face-to-face is lessened, works well for you. Once you've noticed some common themes, you can start tailoring social activities and events to suit you.

In solitude the mind gains strength and learns to lean upon itself.

Laurence Sterne

This is
my journey
and I am
free to choose
my own path

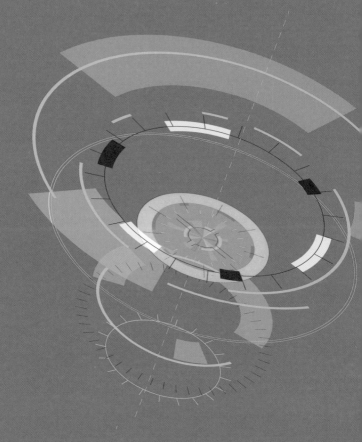

MAKE A MENTAL
HEALTH PLAN

Taking good care of your mental health is important, especially if you are prone to feelings of anxiety or depression associated with loneliness. These problems can take hold fairly quickly, and unless you put some measures in place, they can start to feel overwhelming. The difficulty then becomes breaking the cycle: the worse your mental health gets, the harder it can be to socialize and ask for help, meaning that your loneliness worsens. If you have a history of mental health issues, it can be a good idea to make a plan for how you will cope if your mental health problems start to escalate. During a crisis, it will be difficult to formulate your thoughts around this, so having a clear idea of what you can do beforehand can be useful. Write down your personal action plan – the things you know will help you. For example, who will you contact? Which peer support group can you get in touch with? What small act of self-care could you take to make this period feel more manageable? It's time to make a promise to keep yourself safe.

I WILL NOTICE

AND APPRECIATE

THE KINDNESS

OF STRANGERS

Ways to boost resilience

The term "resilience" refers to how well you handle – and bounce back from – setbacks in your life. Working on building your resilience is paramount when it comes to preserving good mental health. Problems affect us all, but how we handle them can be the difference between sinking into depression and fighting back to become even stronger for it. Developing a more positive outlook by looking for the good in situations; having faith in your abilities; setting realistic but exciting goals; and developing a self-care routine are all good ways to boost resilience.

FORGIVE
YOURSELF
(AND OTHERS)

Holding on to resentment is a sure-fire way to experience mental unrest and even increase social isolation. Constantly berating yourself for past mistakes or holding a grudge against someone else is neither helpful nor constructive. In fact, it is actually damaging and draining. What's more, reliving mistakes or painful past situations over and over in your mind is guaranteed to prolong your suffering, long after the actual moment has passed. You are human, and humans make mistakes. Gently accept your humanness, and the humanness of those around you, by forgiving past behaviours and moving on. Learn from the past, but don't hold onto it. This moment, right now, is a fresh start. Let yourself live free from the shackles of past pain or isolation.

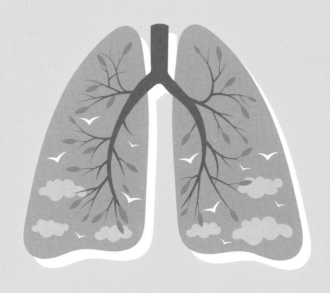

TAKE A DEEP BREATH

Pausing whenever feelings of anxiety start to get overwhelming and taking several long, slow, deep breaths is a centuries-old technique used to help counteract stress. Deep, steady breathing works by interrupting your sympathetic nervous system (which produces the body's "fight, flight or freeze" response) and triggering your parasympathetic nervous system, which invokes a sense of relaxation and calm. It's so simple and effective that you can do it anywhere. Every time you start to feel overwhelmed, anxious, nervous, tense or stressed – for example, in big social situations where you don't yet know anyone – inhale deeply, from the pit of your stomach up to the top of your lungs, then exhale slowly, relaxing your shoulders as you do so. It's beautiful in its simplicity and can allow you to pause mentally for long enough to reassess a situation and figure out how to move forward.

WRITE IT DOWN

Writing down your thoughts and feelings can be incredibly cathartic – the process of putting pen to paper can help to calm your mind, and it may even lend clarity to emotions that you have found difficult to express, or even name. There are many different approaches that you might find helpful – journaling your thoughts, feelings and behaviours in a diary is one method which can help you notice patterns or triggers. You could try writing down the things that have been bothering or upsetting you on pieces of paper, then screwing them up and throwing them away – a physical representation of letting go of negativity. Or try stream-of-consciousness writing, where you have no plan of what to write or where it might take you; you simply start writing whatever comes to mind. These methods can be useful ways of uncovering feelings that you may have been otherwise unwilling to address.

Count to ten

If feelings of isolation are getting on top of you, press pause on your negative thinking. You can quickly interrupt unhelpful thought patterns by taking a deep breath and counting slowly to ten. It might only be a brief respite, but in that short moment you will give yourself a little space and time to calm your mind and counteract the overwhelming sensations you have been experiencing.

TODAY I WILL DO THINGS THAT MAKE MY

soul sing

CULTIVATE POSITIVITY

If you're feeling low, unhappy and isolated, it can be easy to focus solely on daily experiences that reaffirm these emotions and perceptions, until you begin to believe that your life is only made up of negatives. Perhaps you believe that positive people are simply lucky to have completely different daily experiences to you. However, people with an optimistic outlook will still encounter difficult or trying times. It's just that, by seeking out the good things in each and every day, they actively cultivate positivity within their lives, until looking on the bright side has become a habit. To start doing the same, look for positives in ordinary daily activities. Notice the way the sun shines through the clouds as you walk to the shops, or the feel of the hot water on your skin in your morning shower. Think about the most optimistic friends and acquaintances you have – spending a little more time with them could help, even if it's just a quick chat in the office at lunchtime or a phone call one evening. Start choosing happiness – it could brighten your whole outlook.

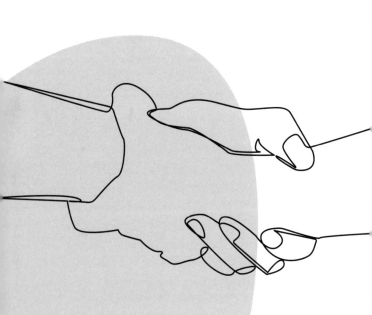

ASK FOR HELP, NOT BECAUSE YOU
ARE WEAK, BUT BECAUSE YOU
WANT TO REMAIN STRONG.

Les Brown

Seeking professional help

If you feel that chronic loneliness is impacting your mental health, it's important to seek help. Talking therapies, such as counselling, can help you unlock any deep-seated beliefs you may hold that are stopping you from forming meaningful relationships and can give you the space you need to discuss your emotions. Cognitive behavioural therapy (CBT) can provide you with practical coping mechanisms to deal with social anxiety, and there are other therapies available. Make an appointment with your doctor to discuss the best option for you.

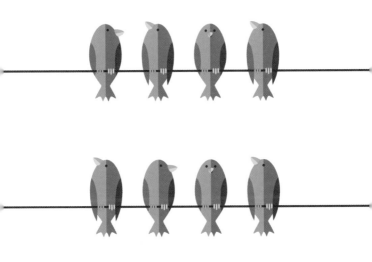

ACCESSING PEER SUPPORT

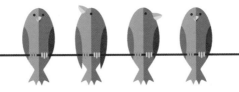

Peer support is when people get together to offer emotional, practical and social support to others going through a similar experience (you might also know them as self-help groups). Peer support provides a valuable network and safe space to share what you are going through and, because you know everyone else in the group has been through a similar experience, you can rest assured you will be listened to and understood. People in the group both offer and receive advice and support. The amount of support you need and are able to provide will likely fluctuate, depending on what you are going through at the time and how new you are to the group. Peer support can be especially effective in helping combat loneliness and related mental health problems, as it offers you the chance to connect and interact. Depending on the group you choose, you may be able to connect online or over the phone, and some local groups may offer face-to-face meet-ups. Check out the resources section at the back of this book to find peer support options.

Be brave

Ultimately, combatting loneliness will mean taking steps to form more meaningful human connections. If you're an introvert, have spent a lot of time alone recently, suffer with social anxiety or another mental health problem or have recently experienced a loss of some kind, making the effort to build a new relationship or strengthen an existing one can seem daunting. But remember: you are a wonderful human being with so much to offer, so be brave... you have nothing to lose!

The snowball effect

Once you've taken those first steps toward building connections with those around you, you will likely find that interacting and forging bonds becomes easier. It's the "snowball effect" – once your plan to reduce feelings of loneliness is underway, it will naturally pick up speed fairly quickly. And once your bonds with others deepen, you will start feeling happier and more fulfilled, creating a positive cycle in your life.

Not everyone will like you, and that's OK

As you start putting relationship-building tips into practice and begin taking steps to form new connections, you will likely find that not everyone responds positively or engages with you – and that's totally normal. Everyone is different, which means some people are simply not going to be your cup of tea – and you won't be theirs. That doesn't mean there is anything wrong with you. It can sometimes be hard accepting this, but there's nothing you can do if you don't gel with someone. Always be yourself, be kind and focus on the people who do like (and love) you.

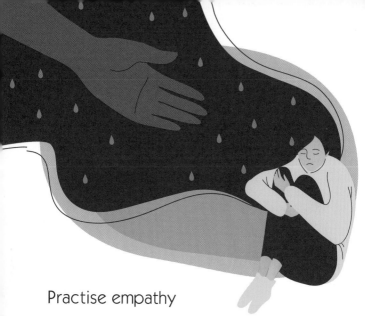

Practise empathy

Everyone knows that being
lonely is not a nice way to feel. If it's something
you have been struggling with recently, you will
have an even deeper understanding of its damaging
effects. So be on the lookout for others who might
be feeling isolated. Notice a friend hasn't been in
contact for a while? Call them and check they're
OK. See a new parent sitting alone in a park?
Smile and say hi. In short, become a champion for
connection and inclusivity!

CONCLUSION

By making small, subtle changes to your everyday habits to help improve your interactions, you will find that your overall happiness and well-being also increase. It's easy to think that it's because something fundamental inside you has changed, but that's not the case. You have always been you, and you have always been a wonderful, valuable human being who deserves joy and happiness, even at times when you haven't felt like it. All that's happened is you've learned a few tricks and tips that have changed your outlook and mindset, boosted your resilience and helped you look on the bright side more regularly. And in doing so, you've hopefully found the inner self-belief needed to reach out to others around you and deepen connections with those closest to you. Continuing to nurture these relationships, as well as making sure you carry on looking after your own health and well-being, will see you go on to make further positive changes in your life, all of which you deserve.

Resources

For further help and information, the following contacts may be useful...

Anxiety and Depression Association of America: Education, training and research into anxiety, depression and related disorders. **adaa.org**

Anxiety UK: This charity provides information, support and understanding for those living with anxiety disorders. **anxietyuk.org.uk**

Befriending Networks: Support for people experiencing loneliness or social isolation. **befriending.co.uk**

CALM: The Campaign Against Living Miserably (CALM) is leading a movement against male suicide. **thecalmzone.net**

Cruse Bereavement Care: Support and information following bereavement. **cruse.org.uk**

Elefriends: A supportive online peer-support community, offering a safe space to listen, share and be heard. **elefriends.org.uk**

Meetup: From book clubs and cookery lessons, to marathon training and hiking holidays, join a local group here! **meetup.com**

Mental Health America: Promoting the overall mental health of all Americans. **mentalhealthamerica.net**

Mind: This mental health charity offers support and advice to help empower anyone experiencing a mental health problem. **mind.org.uk**

National Suicide Prevention Lifeline: Free, confidential support for people in distress in America. **suicidepreventionlifeline.org**

Samaritans: A 24-hour, free, confidential helpline, to support you whatever you're going through. **samaritans.org; 116 123; jo@samaritans.org/jo@samaritans.ie**

Web of Loneliness: Insights, information, resources and practical support to tackle loneliness. **webofloneliness.com**

IMAGE CREDITS

If you're interested in finding out more
about our books, find us on Facebook at
SUMMERSDALE PUBLISHERS and follow
us on Twitter at @SUMMERSDALE.

WWW.SUMMERSDALE.COM